Walking

Stumbling

Limping

Falling

A conversation

Alyson Hallett & Phil Smith

Published by:
Triarchy Press
Axminster, England

info@triarchypress.net
www.triarchypress.net

Copyright © Alyson Hallett and Phil Smith, 2017

The right of Alyson Hallett and Phil Smith to be identified as the authors of this work has been asserted by them in accordance with the Copyright, Designs and Patents Act, 1988.

No part of this publication may be reproduced, stored in a retrieval system or transmitted in any form or by any means including photocopying, electronic, mechanical, recording or otherwise, without the publisher's prior written permission.

All rights reserved

A catalogue record is available from the British Library.

Cover image: 'A Man Who Suddenly Fell Over' by Michael Andrews, oil paint on hardboard, 1952. Reproduced by kind permission of The Estate of Michael Andrews, courtesy of James Hyman Gallery, London: www.jameshymangallery.com

Print ISBN: 978-1-911193-06-7
ePub ISBN: 978-1-911193-07-4

Walking is the art of controlled falling.
                    Robbie Breadon

Dedicated to the memory of Sue Porter.

Contents

Preface 7
Introduction: Alyson 9
A Conversation 13
An Alphabet of Falling: Alyson & Phil 83
Postscript: Phil 89
Appendix 1 94
Appendix 2: Alyson 95
Acknowledgements 97
About the Authors 98

Preface

This is a display copy of a private conversation. Please feel free to have a look.

Over a period of seven months, we exchanged emails that began with a desire to simply communicate with each other about aspects of walking that are not often talked about. We were both becoming acquainted with limping, stumbling and falling in our own lives – sometimes due to illness or injury, at other times due to wearing the wrong footwear or walking on uneven and unfamiliar surfaces.

We had no intention of doing anything with these emails as they were being written, until we were both led onwards by the subjects we were exploring and the delight of being able to explore them. In this sense, the materials we wrote found themselves through the process of writing, and the texts we conceived are collaborative.

There is an introduction by Alyson and a postscript by Phil. In between are the various emails that bounced back and forth between us. At the very end is an alphabet of falling, written by both of us. We hope the book as a whole will expand or distort or unsettle your awareness of what walking is and can be and at the same time extend a community of ambulatory thought and feeling to the concerns and agencies of anyone whose way of walking does not fit the convention of one foot smoothly following the other.

Many of the ideas in this book are in the early stages of formation and as such are prone to leaping from one place to another or progressing abruptly in a way that is closer to a river's meander and flood than an arrow's pursuit of a target. The writing exposes the way our minds were

Preface

working together and we've decided to keep the flow of messiness so that this book becomes the first viewing of a work in progress. Instead of signing off with a name, the writer of each email is flagged up at the beginning of the email along with the date. For the most part we alternate writing with receiving, but this rhythm varies occasionally and stumbles into a different pattern.

If anyone would like to feed into how these provisional ideas might be developed, or would like to invite us to talk more about our explorations, then please get in touch.

Alyson Hallett & Phil Smith
November 2016

Introduction: Alyson

As someone who has always loved walking, it never occurred to me that a day might come when I wouldn't be able to do this. It's not that I'm narrow-minded or without imagination, it's just that walking was stitched into my life in the same way that eating and going to the toilet was stitched into it. It was just something I did. The walk might be anything from a stroll to the Post Office, to a longer trek across hills and fields. Walking helped me to think, it gave rhythm to my movements and thoughts and a sense of being able to move freely through the world.

This changed dramatically four years ago. I didn't have an accident. Nothing terrible happened. I stepped off the train onto the platform at Falmouth Town and suddenly my right leg was hurting. I thought I had pulled a muscle. I visited an osteopath several times but the pain intensified. Eventually I booked a doctor's appointment and asked for an x-ray. There was severe arthritis in my hip joint and the space that should have cushioned the bones had gone.

I plunged into a short-lived depression. Only very old, very decrepit people had to have hip replacements. My life was over. The pain exhausted me. I was irritable. I could no longer solve whatever was troubling me by lacing up my walking boots and setting out for the horizon. Instead, I was stuck on a sofa with a box of tissues and a huge helping of panic and fear. What's more, the pain was in my knee, not my hip, and as I didn't know about referred pain at this point I thought my whole body was crumbling.

Slowly, but surely, I came to accept what was happening with my body. The arthritis was probably caused by the trauma of a road accident that happened when I was nineteen and living in Paris. Who knew why it had decided to come to life and bite me now? But it had and there was nothing I could do except deal with it. Surprisingly, the journey into the depths of crunching bones, limping gaits, major surgery, stumbling and falling has been curious and deeply nourishing.

First off, I became aware of strains of fascism in our cultural perceptions of what constitutes normality in relation to walking. Limping is most definitely not a part of the common picture. Instead of striding or strolling through the town, I now loped from side to side. I moved slowly and painfully. I had to recalibrate every journey: a dash across the road was something I could now only dream of. People looked at me with pity. Some took it upon themselves to tell me I was limping. Some offered to pick me up in their cars because they understood that popping to the other side of town was now a marathon that required pain-killers and a subsequent day of rest to compensate for the massive energy-spend.

Being more sedentary wasn't as bad as I imagined. I read more. I became curious about my hip. I wrote it a letter and asked what it needed. The biggest problem was definitely overcoming my own ideas of what this meant for me. I had been forcibly ejected from normality and now I was standing on the other side – and when I say standing, please picture me as a leaning tower of a human being, always leaning to the left because I was no longer able to distribute weight equally on both legs. Nearly all of my shoes were too heavy and so I wore trainers with everything. Pain came and went – it had tides and moods, it was fickle, illusory, vicious. There were times with friends when I forgot I was in pain. How could that be? How could it disappear so easily when I was distracted? Other times it bit me like a rabid dog. It refused to be calmed or cured. On these occasions, I shrank around it. I withered inwards. I made myself as small as possible and became an island that couldn't move. The weather also affected the bone. Damp weather made it hurt. Hot dry weather eased the pain. It was like a weathervane. All people with bone complaints feel changes in the weather in their skeletal structures and yet conventional medicine refuses to acknowledge this. Why is that?

Contradictions and paradoxes, then, were a large part of this experience for me. I questioned the assumptions of what walking meant. I was annoyed with walking books; walking holidays; walking art; walking for health. Why couldn't we limp for art? Why couldn't we stumble for health? I began to slither in the underbelly of many ideas that I had previously adhered to, that had warmed and comforted me and made me feel a part of things. I remembered doing a sponsored crawl when I was a student at college, being on my hands and knees as I went from Street to Glastonbury only to be thrown out of the George and Pilgrim pub when I arrived because of perceived indecency – whether this referred to the large nappy I was wearing or my refusal to stand up straight I still don't know.

I remembered my piano teacher's black, built-up boot and how he too had always loped from side to side. I loved that boot. It was shiny and bounced up and down like a metronome when I was having lessons. To this day, I hold a special place in my heart for built-up shoes and boots but we rarely see them now. I remembered P.J. Harvey singing about stumbling – and how a ray of light had beamed into my room when I realised stumbling was just as valid a way of moving as any other. I stumble mentally. I totter and fall. I am unstable. Irregular. And here was a singer who was opening a space for this, who was lifting off the intense pressure to appear smooth, to be seen to be moving through the world in a confident and consistent manner.

In some ways, my decrepit hip brought new freedoms. Even though the bones crunched against each other, even though I couldn't walk and was in pain, I felt as if I had entered a new universe. I found a poem by the Brazilian poet Manoel de Barros singing the praises of a man who limps, who creates an irregular and distinct sound as he moves along a road. I slowed down to accommodate the changes my body was visiting upon me. I accommodated the changes, made myself into the kind of country that wasn't frightened of welcoming things it didn't understand, things it might not even like. I sank into my irritability. I was irascible. I read books and watched films instead of going for walks.

Eventually, I stepped forward for surgery and this initiated a whole other trajectory of discovery in my life. Until this happened, though, I was a wanderer in a new land. One of the great things to have emerged from all of this, is the following conversation with Phil Smith. What began as a casual exchange of emails exploring falling, walking, stumbling, became a way of reflecting on experiences that were hard to place in my life and even harder to talk about.

This book examines the ground we walk on, and the way we walk on it. It bounces between personal anecdote and philosophical reflection. It moves in and out of different registers. Sometimes, it too falls flat or plays with an idea that doesn't want to be played with. As I have come to understand it, the ground of our being is physical, spiritual, emotional and mental. I hope our conversation goes some way to exploring this ground and expanding it a little by bringing into play ways of being that we would often prefer not to experience.

A Conversation

24.4.15 From: Phil

At the Walking Artists Network meet-up and symposium in Cornwall last week it was interesting how many challenges there were to the idea of walking as universal and normative – I wonder if we could extend out from limping and put something together that also draws in writing about crawling, tripping, falling, wheeling, and so on?

What do you think?

24.4.15 From: Alyson

I think that's a fantastic idea.

It's really time to break the rather conventional idea of walking – to blow it open.

And yes, let's open it all the way out. Why not?

Stumbling is also one of my favourite things – both metaphorically and in actuality.

Perhaps we can make a dictionary of movement – with 'normal' walking just being one facet of that rather than the dominant paradigm against which other things are often measured?

24.4.15 From: Phil

Brilliant! I like the idea of blowing open walking! So what should we do next?

Would it help if we began with ourselves – that we write stuff that is already in us ... then maybe we could try some anti-normative walks ... separately and together? And then do some writing round those?

There are a number of other potential practitioners/ contributors who we could ask – go walking with and write about that – or ask to join us in writing something. But what do you think? There are downsides to getting lots of contributors ... but a big upside in a multiplicity of voices ... particularly when it's all about anti-normativity!

(See the Appendix on p.94 for details of these people – whose writing is a great companion to this booklet.)

24.4.15 From: Alyson

I think all of those are good ideas –

Let's start with ourselves and writing what we know / have experienced

then let's identify gaps – love the idea of making some walks together as well –

I'm about to have a hip replacement next week so walking is about to become very interesting for me as I learn to walk again –

perhaps we could devise some questions to ask each other as a way of kicking off?

24.4.15 From: Phil

First things first – sending you all best wishes for the op. That's a rather more radical anti-normative journey than I had in mind!

I like your idea of starting with ourselves, then seeing what gaps emerge. And, great, once you're recuperated let's talk about walks, crawls falls together....

Waddling off,

25.4.15 From: Alyson

thanks for the best wishes – much appreciated.

There are really interesting synchronicities around my hip and the world and walking – more details about that later.

Have you read *The Living Mountain* by Nan Shepherd?

Lolloping off,

25.4.15 From: Phil

Nan Shepherd's book is brilliant.... looking forward to your questions

29.4.15 From: Alyson

I'd really like to ask you to write about the experience of learning to walk.

What was that like?

How did it feel?

What happened for you?

If you can't remember, then maybe you can cast yourself back and imaginatively remember?

I think that would be great.

I might answer the question too, as it seems like an important one – and it came to me in a flash when I was eating my porridge today.

29.4.15 From: Phil

Here are three and a half (plus another two quarter) questions for you:

Have you ever fallen, and if so, what it was like and how did it connect/break from your journey before the fall?

If I fell, would you, could you, help me up? And where would that take us? Is there a geography of "up" in walking?

With infinite technology and energy, is there any prosthetic you would wear as you walk?

All bests for your op!

30.4.15 From: Phil

Attaching my first stumbling response to your questions (if I don't do something straight away it tends to get buried....)

Somewhere hidden in a social history, in which I play no part, is a wordless drive to walking on my face; walking composed primarily from percussion. Somehow related to my escape from the wooden cage that will later become forests and old cities. I was kept in there with fabric bears and other hairy things with tight lips. I had somehow piled these monsters into a heap and dragged myself up them, flipping over the bar into a sudden and unexpected empty space between the cot and the carpet.

I found my tender limbs floating down fast, bam, straight on my lip a swinging punch from the whole planet, it split the flesh, but I had so little blood in me then I barely shed a drop, and got on with unfolding the staircase a step at a time.

In my Nan's shop, downstairs, I reigned. I'd tie the whole thing up in wool and cotton. Spinning myself across the linoleum, I somehow open the door, bell rings, my Nan checks but there's no one there, by then.

Turn the volume up; the traffic on the Foleshill Road roars by. No one stops. Maybe no one sees. Pavement slabs spread to the edges of my baby flesh. I sense the gentle incline before it becomes the bump of the canal bridge. I am obsessed by the drive to get somewhere, so I am told, but it will be a long time before the larger shapes have a distracting meaning. I am in the era before stories, shaping my text in worming a parallel line with the busy road. The woman who owns and runs the sweet shop, who through the years will reward me for this moment with sticky things in paper bags, comes, presumably rushing, out to pluck a baby from the pavement slabs.

The buses, trucks and cars play soundtrack. I go straight from crawling to flying.

30.4.15   From: Alyson

here are my responses to your questions:

Have you ever fallen, and if so, what it was like and how did it connect/break from your journey before the fall?

I fell on a concrete floor. It was in my friend's house. We call their house The Ruin. It's not a ruin though, it's an old garage that they've been doing up bit by bit. More of a palace now. The floor was one of the last things they did, so for a long while it was cracked and uneven concrete. One morning, on the way to the bathroom I think, I tripped and fell. The floor was hard. I think I might have been wearing my black jogging pants – they're a bit flared – sometimes they trip me up. I felt a fool. And it hurt. I stood up and wandered around. My friends were worried. I wasn't at that point. I can't remember if I carried on to the bathroom or not. I think I sat on the sofa. My friends went out to work. My leg hurt from the fall and so I decided that I needed to get it checked out. I was in London, Deptford. I wasn't registered with a doctor because I was visiting. I decided to visit the local A&E in Lewisham. It was quite a long way there, but I thought it was worth it. The more I walked, the less my leg hurt. By the time I got to Lewisham it didn't hurt at all and so I didn't go to the hospital. Instead, I went into a shopping centre and rummaged around in TK Maxx. I love that shop. I bought a pair of shoes. I still haven't ever worn them to this day.

If I fell, would you, could you, help me up? And where would that take us? Is there a geography of "up" in walking?

My friend, I would do whatever I could to help you up. I'd ask first, to see if you wanted to get up again. There was a time, once, when I saw a man in a gutter in Glasgow. I thought he needed help. I went over to him and said hello, is there anything I can do? He told me to fuck off. He was having a good snooze in the gutter and didn't want to be disturbed by a do-gooder. So, if you said yes, you'd like some help getting up, then I'd see what I could do.

So much would depend upon how much weight I could bear.

You are bigger than me and it's unlikely that I could bear all of your weight.

If I found that I wasn't strong enough, then I'd enlist some other people to help with the task of getting you up after falling. We'd do whatever it takes to get you into the place where you want to be.

When we manage this, we will all be standing.

It will be a small journey where we have had to navigate the vertical plane rather than the horizontal plane. We will all be standing, some of us taller or shorter than the others. It will have taken our heads up higher. It will have taken our bodies further away from the earth. It will have raised our heads up on our necks, we will be balancing again on our little feet. And even if our feet are big, they always seem so little in comparison with how much of us is upright.

Is there a geography of up?

Is there a mountain?

Is there a hope, a desire?

Is there a leap?

Is there a top of a wardrobe?

Is there a stair to climb?

Is there a bed to get out of?

Is there a bird in the sky to look at?

Is there an exercise for lengthening your spine?

Relax, we all get taller when we relax.

Is there a geography of up?

Is there a map of the sky – where it begins and where it ends?

With infinite technology and energy, is there any prosthetic you would wear as you walk?

A tail. I would like to have a tail. I would wear it at the bottom of my coccyx. It would swish around. It would be great for balancing when I'm teetering along a narrow pole. It would be quite a sleek tail. I'd have to have my trousers retailored. A little hole at the back for the tail to peek out. Imagine all the things I could do with a tail. Cats and dogs, monkeys and pumas – they'd never look at me in the same way again.

1.5.15   From: Alyson

Today is the day I have my hip replacement operation, the day when a surgeon will saw off the femoral head of my right femur and insert a prosthetic head in its place. There is no pre-med. I am rather disappointed about this. I pull on tight, white, knee-length socks and wait with my friend Roz for a porter to arrive. The waiting seems to go on forever. And then there's a knock on the door. This is it. IT. I take a deep breath and start to lie down, only to be told to get off the bed. Off the bed? Yes. In this hospital you walk behind the bed to the operating theatre. The porter manoeuvres the bed out of the door, I hug my friend goodbye, and walk. It is strange and surreal this last walk with my arthritic hip. People smile and wave at me. They know where I'm going. I know where I'm going too. I am walking to a theatre where I will be made unconscious, cut open, sawn, hammered, stitched back together. Every step I take involves a conscious choice. I hadn't expected to be doing this. I had expected to be wheeled along in a bed. Each step I take now, each limping step is important. This is the last time I will ever walk with my own right hip inside of me.

13.5.15 From: Phil

I hope your operation went OK – I've seen that you've been active on FB so i'm hoping that is a good sign!

I'm going largely out of contact for a couple of weeks in the wilds of Milton Keynes, but I'll keep in mind your questions while I'm there and keep writing.

Until I do, a further question for you:

Once I sat at a desk and couldn't move. Can you write anything about that desk?

31.5.15 From: Alyson

An interesting thing about recovering from a total hip replacement operation is the way in which each of my legs are now referred to by professionals. I no longer have a right and a left leg, but a good leg and an unoperated leg. Of course, when they refer to the good leg without mentioning the other one, a part of my brain assumes that the other leg is in fact the bad leg because these binaries / dualities are so deeply embedded. Along with this grasping of my brain comes a strange and rather subtle sense of sadness; poor bad leg, what has it gone and done now? And a certain annoyance with the good leg – how has it achieved this accolade, what goodness has it performed that the other leg hasn't been able to?

Now, you may be wondering what this has to do with you at your desk. Well, here's what I'm thinking: a desk is a place that's associated with work, and often with being at school. I thought you had written that you were at school when you sat at a desk and couldn't move. I made that up – or, my brain once again took a short associative route to the easiest desk connection it could find.

Desks, though, are different to tables. We don't – on the whole – sit around a desk to eat. We don't go to a desk to relax. We go to a desk to carry out a work task, whether we are at school or at work or generally foutering around with a task that needs doing.

For now, I'd like to stay with the school desk which is, always and forever it seems, a place where we receive news not only of fascinating information but also of what is right and what is wrong. What is good and what is bad (just to clarify the leg connection here). This introduction to binaries tends to be fundamental to the schooling process. As a child, then, we can be in the throes of a great passion – for chemistry, for physics, for storytelling, for drawing – when, quite often, we will be suddenly halted the way a train can be halted by an obstacle in its path. This halting is brought about by the sudden knowledge that our absorption is no longer just a wholesome immersion in something that fascinates us, but that it is also part of a judgement system, one where there is a very definite right and a very definite wrong. For an immersed and immersive brain, this moment is cataclysmic. It ends the world as we knew it. It introduces an idea that has not arisen within us, but has been imposed from without.

Right and wrong. And along with this, there come rewards and punishments. Right is on the side of good, and thus deserves a reward. Wrong is on the side of bad, and thus deserves a punishment.

I therefore think that the time you sat at a desk and couldn't move was due to the fact that your body/brain experienced an echo, a reminder of that first moment when you were wrenched from absorption and rudely hurled into a world of duality that made no sense to your imagination, no sense to the way you were, no sense to the world as you lived in it. This moment was a trauma, and the subsequent paralysis was an expression of this, an appropriate response to the shattering of life as you knew it.

My question for you is this: with a prosthetic hip, am I more or less human?

12.6.15 From: Phil

As I would expect, you are unusually perceptive. It was a school desk. Equally, I find your thesis entirely convincing.

Your question:

You have a weird industry in you:
Alloys, fierce processes and plans,
To dance around all your dead stars.
Unnaturally smooth and full of jags,
Running at various velocities, and
Already carrying your monument,
More natural than you have ever been:
You have more history, museum, stuff;
Precision tooled, you are
No longer too human, and near enough.

An email from Amy Sharrocks has made me think about falling – about my Dad dying just under a year ago as a result of a fall. How I am more careful now. How I often feel, when out walking alone, in obscure places, not wild places, but ditches and verges and the innards of roundabouts that people very rarely visit, that if I were to fall there, no one would come, no one would hear. In some sense, are they fallen places; fallen outside of human use. Or is this their transfiguration, their come-to-placeness?

Are there falling places? Injuring places? Are there places that are waiting for a limping gait?

Best wishes,

15.6.15 From: Alyson

thanks so much for this response.

I'd really like you to say more about your dad falling. How that affected him. How that affected you.

And then, more about these falling places. Open it up a bit. Tell me more. I'm intrigued and moved.

23.7.15 From: Phil

A fall for a person, like my Dad, with fairly severe dementia – you begin to sense just how fragile the fragile body is – how quickly a body that seems good for living can turn on a person, how the virtuous cycling of materials and flows of liquids can begin to poison the body as it seeks to save one part of itself at the expense of another, and as the clinicians fire-fight from organ to organ, unable to halt the wild plunging from one trough to another.

The places. I immediately think of a walk I took, at low tide, along a part of the river bed of the Teign. I was enjoying myself finding odd things on the bed and immediate bank, but at one point there was an appealing path cutting away and up and I took it. I climbed and within seconds I found myself on a tiny path a few inches wide with a straight 40-foot drop to the rocks below. I suddenly felt my relaxed wander sharply focus to one of survival; no leeway for a loose step, a loss of balance would be to lose everything. My happy contemplation of the rot and ruin of metal landing stages, a surprise shrine to the Buddha, what I thought was a fossil that turned out to be a fragment of bathroom tile with a fossil design, suddenly took on the feeling of a winding down to a full stop, a last chorus. I clung to the side of the rise and edged my way along, scraping my body across the rock, until the land fell away to a field and then a pub. It was a strange and sudden rising up of the possibility of a fall.

But the second place I think of is more of a 'fallen' than a 'falling' place. It was behind a sports centre, I can't remember what town now, but I think it was Taunton, heavily wooded overhead, with the ground tangled in mire, dark roots, twisted metal, faded litter that spoke of a human retreat which itself had been abandoned, and everything in the dark shadow melding into the same dark bluish-grey. The rank dankness of it was hard on the skin and throat, my chest shrank back from it; wanting its sanctuary it wanted none of me. I scrambled out through closed bushes and branches, and fell onto the service road. Shambling away I surprised a member of staff having a smoke and realised how in her eyes I was a zombie emerging from shadows, the lost returning damaged to the world, an outsider coloured the same dark bluish-grey as the sanctuaries no one visits.

My question for you: if there are 'good' and 'bad' legs, are there fallen places?

Best wishes,

1.8.15 From: Alyson

many thanks for your beautiful and moving reflections.

Are there fallen places?

The first thing that came into my mind was a time when falling was an instinctive thing to do.

I was in Taunton. I had just driven there from North Devon to meet a friend. There is a particular alleyway I was entering when my phone rang. I really like that alleyway. It's where I had a ring made when I was eighteen; part of it is lined with funky, interesting shops, the other part is more like an empty corridor. I answered my phone and was told that an old friend, an old lover, had died. Before I knew what was happening I slumped to the ground.

I don't know if I fell or if the ground swooped up to catch me.

But there I was. In a part of the alleyway where men pissed at night against the wall and now my back was against that pissy wall and my legs were curled under me.

Is this a fallen place? A place where I found permission to fall?

Standing up was not an option. The world fell away and I fell with it. Everything known had changed. If I had been in a more public place, somewhere tidier, posher, could this have happened? Maybe not. I love that fallen place and I hate it too. It allowed me to absorb some of the shock. It took me into itself. It gave no shelter.

Is Euston Station a fallen place? Has anyone had a happy time there? I read recently that when it was first built, farmers staged a big protest because they didn't want their fields to be translated into metal train tracks. They didn't want the green to be bitten into by shades of grey, they wanted the sky to be kept open. They wanted space to be kept as space rather than hemmed in. Later, the station was the site of an IRA bomb. Later still, I fell there. I was walking through it when a memory hit me in the belly. Fifteen years previously I'd come to this station from an island I was living on in Scotland. My lover should have been there to meet me but he wasn't. He was away with another woman in Wales. I didn't fall over when I found that out, but fifteen years later when I happened to be in the station again. It was as if the building had stored the memory for me and suddenly redelivered it – the pain and the shock, the disbelief, the tears. I fell out of time that day, snatched into the past the way the wind can snatch a hollow-boned bird and fling it this way and that. I fell down and now, for me, that station is a fallen place. It cannot be redeemed. Sorrow is etched into it and not just by me.

(Note from Phil: How strange. In the mid-1970s on occasional visits to London I would walk across the large concourse at Euston Station feeling very vulnerable to a bombing; these were existential moments of aloneness in a vast modern expanse. On a student theatre tour of Somerset villages in 1975, I bought a pair of Second World War leather despatch rider boots from a kindly shopkeeper. Shortly afterwards, crossing the Euston concourse in my new boots, the nails in the soles slid on the smooth tiles and I went crashing to the ground.)

Fallen places, fallen people. Each time we are reminded of fragility, there's a falling. I wonder if there are places then where the earth expresses its fragility? Its fallenness? I have lived with crumbling cliffs, but these were not fallen places. The most fallen place I have been to is Leverndale psychiatric hospital. Not the land that has fallen, but the things that have been built on that land. I can't think of one place that in itself is fallen. The earth is indifferent to falling and rising. It doesn't care to rise and fall. It rises and falls all the time – mountains, cliffs, coastal paths – but it doesn't have a feeling about this. That's what we bring to the equation.

Please can you tell me about a bad walk. Where you were going. What made it bad. How you came to think of it in this way.

And I had a rather ridiculous idea – slightly dangerous – a place we might walk in – but a bit nervous to even write it down....

hope all is well,

13.8.15 From: Phil

A bad walk?

I remember a bad bit of a walk somewhere between Teignmouth and Oddicombe, when I front-loaded the route with mini-performances and exhausted the audience and the material too quickly, so that the second half of the journey became ramble like, and took too long. People had places to get to in the evening, it was getting late, we were eight miles from our starting point, to which I'd promised we'd return, and I'd hoped to have time at Oddicombe to introduce them to Oddie (a human hot dog pouring mustard on his head), it turned everything functional, anxious ... there is a happy ending to this tale, but that was a partially bad walk.

I was taken on a walk in Manchester where we were guided by a map of somewhere else. This was repeatedly presented as a novelty, as somehow revelatory, but it very quickly became a repetitious discordance all the more dispiriting for its unintended parody of playfulness. I began to despair of disrupted walking, and felt the thin border between revelation and whimsy. That was a bad walk.

I remember a 'bad' walk I was taken on by two of my students during which I was blindfold, seized by both arms, and raced at great speed across a square, placed against what had been a bomb shelter and then had large lumps of concrete lobbed at the wall around me as I semi-cowered, semi-trusted to the flow of what was happening. This was witnessed by our sister class on the same module who asked their tutor if they could do the same to him. That was a "badass" walk.

Maybe I should never know of your ridiculous, slightly dangerous idea?

What about the moment one lifts oneself up or is lifted up from a fall, or what about getting up from the ground to walk?

14.8.15 From: Alyson

I want to tell you about a time when I picked myself up off the ground and walked. Telling you this means entering a blind space, one that I can't quite see.

It was October, Paris, 1983. I was a student living at Cité Universitaire on the southern outskirts of the city. I needed to go to the local supermarket and buy food. To get there, I had to cross the road. I was careful, took my time and waited for the green man. It's easy to forget that cars are coming from a different direction, what can feel like the wrong direction when you're abroad. When the green man appeared I started to walk and then I was aware of something on my left, a buzzing thing, a metal thing on wheels coming straight for me. The motorcycle crashed into me and I fell heavily on my right side. I remember the sound of my skull hitting the tarmac. It's odd to write this as I feel as if I'm blind and can see at the same time. Going into the blind, unrememberable space means relying upon imagination as well as memory. I know I was run over, but I don't know if it was a motorcycle or a moped.

I stood up. The man on the motorcycle had fallen too. He stood up. I picked up his helmet and asked if he was okay. I think people asked me if I was okay. I said yes, I am fine. The man got back on his motorcycle and drove away. I finished crossing the road, went to the supermarket and bought potatoes and washing-up liquid. I then went back to my room.

When I got to my room, I sat on my bed and thought, I've just been run over. Then I started to shake. I shook for a long time. I don't remember what I did next.

Another fall came to me just four days before I was due to leave the UK and go travelling for the first time. I was staying with my sister and we had gone to climb the Isle of Frogs (Brent Knoll) at sunset with her three children. It was a great climb up. I could see the Severn Estuary, Burnham, Weston-Super-Mare glittering in the distance. At the top, I took off my shoes and rambled around. I've always liked to walk in bare feet. To feel the grass under them, the tickle of earth and stones.

As we began our descent I put my shoes back on. I didn't want to slip. And then I slipped and fell down and as I hit the ground I heard something crack. My wrist started to swell. Just a sprain, I said. But it hurt. It was painful. My sister helped me to stand up again. Her hand coming down to share the weight of my body as we heaved it from the horizontal plane back to the vertical one. I couldn't have done it without that hand. Her hand was my invitation. My ticket back to the world of the standing.

We went to the A&E department in Weston. They x-rayed my arm and sure enough I'd fractured my wrist.

Breaking my wrist just days before I was due to travel to Canada was problematic. I discovered that my travel insurance would not cover me when I was abroad because the accident happened before I left the UK. This meant that any treatment I needed when I was away would have to be paid for. I was very worried about this as I didn't have much money and given that I'd be gone for 3 months, I'd need my cast removed and x-rays to check the bone had healed.

The doctor who put a purple, fibreglass cast on my arm was Canadian. He encouraged me to go on my travels and assured me things would work out in one way or another.

I was comforted and emboldened by his words and so one warm, autumn morning a friend drove me to Heathrow and I set off into the unknown with a fractured wrist to see what would happen. Practically, this meant ditching half of my clothes before leaving as I couldn't wear them over the cast. It meant asking people on the plane to help me open my plastic-wrapped portion of cheese because I couldn't do it with one hand. It meant asking for a bottom bunk when I checked into each youth hostel as I couldn't climb a ladder to a top bunk.

I slowed everything down. Travelled up to Tadoussac and decided to stay there for two weeks to give myself a chance to heal and get used to having a fractured arm. I walked differently with my arm in a cast. I was wounded. I was more careful. I didn't try to do too many things, especially to begin with.

And then I got a bit braver. I went on longer walks. I went out in a very small boat to see whales. I could only hold on with one hand and as the boat bounced in and out the waves I thought I was going to be thrown into the sea. I yelled to be taken back to harbour, then I saw a whale and forgot all about my own fragility. The size of the thing. The immense grandeur of it. I held on tightly with my one hand and said silent prayers and hoped we'd all get back to land alive.

Next, I went to Toronto to see a friend. I walked around the city each day, visited the library, spent hours and hours listening to Glenn Gould recordings. After a week or so, I decided to move on and ended up making a 7-day road trip with a complete stranger that I met through a ride-share scheme. We drove from Toronto into the USA, then from east to west along long, long roads. We slept in the car. Ate food from tins. I even drove for a hundred miles or so but it wasn't easy turning the wheel with a cast on.

Along the way I decided not to go back to Canada and headed to Portland, Oregon instead. I checked into a youth hostel and spent the best part of a week wandering around, visiting Powell's City of Books, reading in cafés, heading out to Canon Beach.

A Conversation

When it was nearly time to get my cast taken off I went to a neighbourhood medical centre and sat there with the drunks and the prostitutes, with all the other people who didn't have medical insurance. A nurse (?) took my details then took my pulse with her thumb not her finger. I started to feel a mild level of panic. What was I doing here? Maybe I should keep the cast on for 3 months instead of the recommended 6 weeks? Maybe I should find a sawmill and ask them to saw the cast off?

I was referred to a hospital and given an appointment for 7 in the morning in two days' time. I set off early, on buses, heading out to a big hospital on a hill. I checked in then sat in a giant armchair and watched fishes swimming around in an aquarium. It was more like a hotel than a hospital.

The doctor who saw me that day was Scottish. Hearing his voice was a joy. He was warm and friendly. He treated me with great respect and attention. I was x-rayed, given a sling, then sent on my way again without being asked to pay a single dollar for my treatment.

Are there angels in this world?

Yes, there are angels in this world.

Angels are all the kind people who come to help us.

Now, my next question for you is: what is the most special walk you have made with another person. Was the place already special? Did you make it special? Would it have been possible to fall in a place, at a time, like that?

28.9.15 From: Phil

I had a thought about falling. It connects to Tomas Espedal's words about walking on tarmac roads in *Tramp*. He is very damning of that experience and of the material of the tarmac road. Yet, while acknowledging the toll they take on joints and muscles, the odd hammering of oneself against the surface, I have always enjoyed the freedom that the smooth surfaces gives me for looking up. On uneven ground there are the constant little trips from eccentric stones. I had this all the way walking up Cap Fréhel in Brittany the other day, and there is a sort of wearing pleasure in being nudged every few seconds with one's fragility, one's conditionality, to be all the time on the edge of a fall, tipping one's frame forward and weighing it. Yet, I also like the smooth road surface; to be taking advantage of the invasive traffic structure, to gaze over hedges, into people's homes, across fields, up to the flights of birds and satellites.

I have been limping with my neck. For about a month now the connection between my head and the rest of my body is in mechanical disruption. It is an old injury, from more than 30 years ago. I dug for a few hours using the wrong action, bending my neck, a contribution to a City Farm for giving a young people's football team free use of their pitch.

Maybe it's older than that – slouching, unwilling or unable to present myself to the world, pulling the vertebrae out of position. I've been able to feel the misalignment for years, occasionally my neck would freeze for a day or two and then free up again. This time it froze, freed up, but remained painful in a new way, creating sheets of white and silvery pain, sharp and bright, blinding, sucking all thought onto the edge of its blade, sometimes spasming the muscles around it so I would have to stop and try to slowly unlock everything.

Anti-inflammatory tablets took the edge off the pain, but no cure, so I have been visiting a chiropractor and I can feel how the bones are now in a different alignment thanks to his cracking and shoving. Things are not resolved but something is happening. A part of my neck/back that has been stuck for thirty years has begun to move. But the consequences ripple up and down me, nothing is stable, nothing is cured, there is no return to the not-having-to-think-about-it of before.

I am divided, the ghost of Descartes has appeared as a surgeon, a royal axeman, there are negotiations at the borders of head and body, prisoners are exchanged.

While exploring around and beyond the boundaries of the Royal William Victualling Yard in Plymouth, making a performance walk, I ventured down some steps covered in a green slime. I walked carefully down them. And stopped. Then, not as if by any continuation of my motion, my legs shot out in front of me and I began to fall through my spine towards the rock of the steps. My elbows shot back and my skeleton assumed the shape of a cage, my forearms slamming down onto the steps, but protecting my skull from slamming back into the sharp corners of the steps. I'd taken a little skin from a finger and for years I could feel a tiny piece of bone that was loose in my elbow. A bony chip in fluid. If I forgetfully leaned upon it the pain was big and sudden and I would jerk up from it. In the performance walk I invited the audience to feel this floating chip of bone, to consider my body as a geometrical cage and compare it to the symmetry of the Yard (which I later revealed to be my lie and its illusion).

I'm never very good with any kind of ranking – favourite film, most special place, however....

As part of the long walk I wrote about in *On Walking*, I wandered for a day with Ivan Cutting, a friend from university who had set up Eastern Angles Theatre Company and kept it alive for 30 or more years (it's still going) – an extraordinary achievement and a gift to the community from which he had come, in some ways an indictment of my professional nomadism: a jobbing writer having to conjure from nowhere loyalty to each new project; on the road often, disconnected, living in spare rooms, a shed once, hostels, B&Bs ... the walk was special for its doubleness, it was part of the journey of W. G. Sebald's that I was copying, it was doubled by Ivan, it was doubled again by his intense and detailed knowledge of the land around us and my curious ignorance, it was doubled by my writing it all down inside my head as went along. We did not fall, but we slithered across a clay-like beach beneath eroding cliffs, sticky and uneven, with a tide rapidly coming in, deciding we would risk it, a choice we knew we would hate our children to make. We were fine, and Ivan was on his home territory, I was the stranger; surely he would have some secret local knowledge that would open up the cliff face, would lift us to the top and out of the waves; he knew of the secret auxiliary units so why not the secret routes out of physics?

I can't remember now if I wrote to you of my work-in-progress performance as part of the DIY workshop on walking led by Nando Messias in Plymouth – as part of this I would throw myself to the ground (in Plymouth shopping centre) having placed a cardboard sheet on the ground in preparation.

Can you invent some scores for falling (or throwing yourself down) performances? Or maybe a poem for speaking having fallen or thrown yourself down?

I follow your adventures a little on FB! Keep well,

11.11.15 From: Alyson

I like that idea, scores for falling down performances,
poems that can be read when you are fallen
or when you have thrown yourself down.

Following my hip operation, I have been paranoid about falling over. In my mind, I have reckoned that as soon as I fall my new hip will dislocate and I will be back to point zero. Needing more surgery and starting the whole lengthy process all over again. Because of this belief I have avoided muddy ground, my caution has gone out before me wherever and whenever I have been walking. A safe walker, a mind rooted in staying upright, so much depending upon the body remaining vertical unless I gave it permission to be otherwise.

I was consciously avoiding accidents – and that was exhausting – wanting to be in control all the time to avoid anything bad happening. How small that makes me. How constricted.

One time I fell on the isle of frogs and broke my wrist – that was a long time ago – and just two days before i went travelling. I can't remember if I've told you that story – if I haven't, then let me know.

The Butoh practitioner and founder – Kazuo Uno – is in my mind a lot. He lived with pigs for ten years in a pig pen. A lot of time spent on the ground, in with their trotters and shit. Down there where you can't really fall any further. The atom bomb had exploded and there was no way he could go back to a dance form that was all about looking beautiful, creating shapes with the body, appearing to be perfect. He returned to the ground and the earth and the shit and started working from there. Working with what became known as 'a frog's-eye view'.

At the beginning of September I was in Hartland, North Devon. I went out early one sunny morning and walked to Saint Catherine's Tor. Only half the Tor is there, the other half has been scooped into the sea. Dissolved. Swept away. I love that place. There's a flat field behind the Tor that was a swannery. No swans now, just the echo of them, a hint of swan in the green field by the sea. I walked to the Tor and stared out at Speke's beach. Lots of rocks, ribs of rocks spanning out to sea and huge Atlantic rollers pouring in. I was wearing an old pair of Birkenstock sandals. I felt a bit reckless and I was enjoying that. There were a couple of other walkers in huge boots, waterproofs, laden down with maps etc. and there I was in my clapped-out sandals, shorts and a t-shirt. I felt a bit smug – especially because this is where I used to live and so, in some secret way, I feel very connected to this land, some sense of being more bonded to it than walkers who are doing the coast path, just passing by and glancing. I was on the moral high-ground then, a little lifted inside myself, a little eagle in her pompous eyrie. Heading back towards the car-park I started to walk the down hill that's just inches from the edge of the cliff – and slipped and fell. It happened very quickly. One minute I was upright, the next I was tumbling down. I landed softly, and laughed. I laughed so much because I was relaxed, because pride really had come before my fall, because I enjoyed the falling. Plus, my hip hadn't dislocated. My hip was just fine. It was in place, the muscles had reunited enough to hold it there. I didn't need to go to hospital and have surgery. I was just a fallen woman and in that moment a fallen woman was a great and liberating thing to be. My hands were grazed on the gravel, but those grazes were trophies. I went back to my friend's house and regaled her with my joyful falling tale.

I have fallen once again since then, on mud this time, and again the same sense of mirth. The delight in not finding myself broken – although it has been pointed out to me that I probably don't want to make a habit of doing this.

Once, when I lived in Hartland, I listened to a P.J. Harvey song, and she sang about stumbling. At least I think she did. But I remember being intrigued by this, by foregrounding ways of walking and being that are not sure-footed. I liked that. To stumble. To stutter. To topple. To tremble. To stagger. So many ways of moving – and yet so much work connected with walking doesn't seem to explore the wide vocabulary of how a walk can happen. When I had my arthritic hip, I came to see this as part of the fascism of normality – there is a good healthy walk, and there is a limp. If you are a limper – and I was – you are also a bit of a leper, someone who doesn't fit, someone outside of the castle whose ramparts are guarded by the good, healthy walkers who have two legs that are the same length and two hip joints that are not being eaten by arthritis. I hadn't been aware of this before. But my limp took me into a new world.

I haven't written a score for falling – but I'd like to. I will think more about this. I don't know what the score would look like.

Today, I wore my walking boots for the first time in two and a half years. With an arthritic hip, the boots were too heavy and so they have bumbled around in the boot of my car for all of this time. They were a bit mouldy. But they felt amazing. I walked to a hill opposite my house and kept saying to Craig, my friend, I'm wearing my walking boots! I'm wearing my walking boots! It is a monumental day today for this reason. For the simple fact that I can wear my boots again. I love those boots.

Like you, I also love to walk on tarmac sometimes. It allows for an uninterrupted rhythm. A kind of glissando, a pace and scale that flows. Whereas field, hill, mountain walking is more staccato, more cautious because it contains the potential for a fall.

I loved what you wrote in your last mail. I want to know more about your neck. The description of pain was amazing. Let's look at what happens to pain when we walk. What happens to pain when we talk back to it.

18.11.15   From: Phil

I have been limping with my whole body. Just as damage to, say, an ankle might hold back a leg so that in each step that leg drags, pulling the stride back or pushing it abruptly upwards, breaking the rhythm, so for the past two months my whole body has been fighting an unidentified infection, spasmed in bouts of coughing and dragging itself into exhaustion.

At first I tried to carry on as if nothing was happening, and the pause in the life-limp became long sleeps of nine, ten and eleven hours, followed by revival and onto the next project.

But I caught something else, some common infection, on top of the original infection, and had to stop. And now I have been mostly sitting or lying, chained by this limp to beds, chairs and sofas.

Sweat streams down me in an hour or two of gentle fever then subsides and leaves the delta of my head clear for a few hours work, or watching or reading.

I am a lobster moulding itself to the niche in which it is caught. The tail trying to wag the dog. The parasite waiting in the sofa to attach itself to some passing idea, no longer able to frame its own furniture.

I get smaller as I cram into the thin crevice. Squashed out of shape, I notice which ideas return and which are hungry to get away. There is a kind of rationalisation, based on wanting, in process.

A Conversation

A poem for reading when you fall down:

> This is the view from a cardboard mattress,
> The barely registered point of no return.
> This is the lizard level, boxes stacked cock-eyed in a corner,
> Heads in spit, you are at rock bottom.
> The gutter of a star from where no one looks up.
> Welcome to the lowest of the low, beneath the underdog,
> Worthy of zombie humanism and redemption.
> Like a child spiked on a thin slab of good,
> Lain where dust is an imperial waste ground,
> And carpet wrinkles are ranges and valleys
> That hammer into the skirting boards.

A poem on having thrown myself down:

> These, me, are the foothills of my father's garden,
> Red clay trenches and front lines in the struggle for purity
> Where excess oozes out from between the bricks
> Like slug's innards.
> These are the dusty battlefields where Corgi and Dinky
> Were converted among the vegetables.
> These, me, are where you learned to radicalise yourself,
> Deploying embarrassment strategically.
> These, me, are the parade grounds of shame.
> Here the church organist designed amphibian vehicles and the neighbours
> Papered over their windows with newsprint. Here, garden fires

And rust cut through the fences, and we, kids, me and the now dead to me,
Invaded our allies, and at night stole through the gardens we had played in
During the day. These are the soils that have been swept away,
The flesh that never had bones in them, anyway.

Is there anything to be said for your walking with "caution ... gone out before me"? Anything that that reveals?

Yes, you told me about the Isle of Frogs.

When you wrote "just inches from the edge of the cliff.... I was tumbling down" – I had empathic vertigo for you, though I know you cannot have fallen from the cliff, such is my desire, a desire that is fixed by a hook deep into a part of my pelvis, a desire that shrivels me with its parody of want, to be leaping, flying. I had to pin myself against the back of my chair so I would not cause you to fall.

The limper as leper. This is the stultifying and imperative insistence of *for your own good, to walk or else!* And to work within the norms. To walk with purpose, destination, to walk away from obesity, to walk away from heart disease, to walk into gainful employment, to walk yourself into a workable capital, to generate a surplus, to walk like a pen within the box and between the lines, to walk straight for the police officer, to walk soberly, non-provocatively, with face raised to the CCTV, unhooded, cowed but un-cowled.

"more topple" – the boots I have worn for some years now, while cushioning the blows to my knees, are not great on wet stone ... so after rain, although for some strange reason – although I almost never check a weather report – I very rarely walk in the wet, I walk with a crouching insectoid gait, making two legs into six somehow, short steps, soles flat to the rising ground, holding onto rails and walls.

Walking in pain, walking with blisters (before applying plasters) when the pressure on the nerve endings is taut and sharp, is a meditative act, divine sparks sailing above a body-botched-by-a-demiurge, until the two, body and consciousness, become partners; the mystical walks beside the suffering. I never thought anything worthwhile during these walks in pain, but I survived, and I associate that kind of self-preservation in pain as being-degree-zero, not noble or revelatory, and that whatever is worthwhile comes through pleasure.

Is there something to be written about walking carefully that goes beyond safety?

20.11.15 From: Phil

Ill Walking Day 1

Walking back through the volcanic arch and veering right down the hill, the slippery road with a mulch of leaves underfoot bears left and frames, in the dark masses of the trees I fear will in one night of storms fall and kill us in our beds, two cubes of the modernist houses that stand opposite our house. White, they shimmer against the distant green hills and the thick trunks of the rare cedars; yet they are not complete, despite their symmetry, their relation is still dynamic, the first slightly edgy with the second. There are things left to do.

On the pavement in the close, having waded through dead leaves piled like corpses in history, two small branches have been blown from a tree. They, unevenly mirroring each other. I step carefully over this pair of accidental antlers. I know from where they have come: *Helen's Story* by Rosanne Rabinowitz, a riff upon Machen's *The Great God Pan*. The two stories square up to each other on the street. The lichen stares saucer-eyed. I am using my headache as a means to tie with frayed steel hawsers these fragments from the sedentary day. The being alongside.

Best wishes,

20.11.15 From: Alyson

the being alongside
how much do I love that?
It reminds me of the St Patrick breastplate prayer:

Christ be with me, Christ within me,
Christ behind me, Christ before me,
Christ to comfort and restore me.
Christ beneath me, Christ above me,
Christ in quiet, Christ in danger,
Christ in hearts of all that love me,
Christ in mouth of friend and stranger.

A Conversation

I have no idea why – I suppose I like this naming of places that are very close to us that usually get overlooked. What's alongside or just behind, rather than out there on the horizon, or in some country far away.

Sometimes what's closest to us can be furthest away.

My dad, for instance, is so close to me at the moment and yet he couldn't be further away either. No longer alive, he's left this world, but because he lived here and because his memories live in me he couldn't be nearer. These paradoxes are so important, so painful, so crucial.

Just tonight I walked up to the mast on top of the Mendips. I don't know why I did that. I pulled my car over and walked up to the great steel totemic needle that points into the sky. This is the mast of my childhood – the great finger that has pointed into the sky for as long as I've been alive. It brought me Doctor Who when I was a child, and John Peel, all things that were important to me that came through the television or radio.

How many nights have I seen its little red light flashing? How many times have I driven past it or been driven past? It's as much a part of my life as my elbow.

So tonight, the air laced with an icy chill, I walked up to the great beast. It's monstrous, huge, it hums, there are great wires anchoring it to earth, as if it might suddenly take off or topple over. There were bullocks in the field around it – we were disinterested in each other. And then I glimpsed a trig point so I walked over to it and the whole of the Somerset Levels laid themselves out beneath me. I gasped. I called my dad's name over and over again. This land, this great county is so full of my family I can't look at it without seeing them all there, in the mist, in the fingers of sun that poked through a cloud, in the coasts, in the solid and distant cube of Hinkley Point nuclear power station, in the rhynes, in the fields. And then Glastonbury Tor and just on from it Butleigh monument, the place where my father went on the day that his father died. Suddenly there was an almost straight line between these three points: the mast on top of the Mendips where I was saying the goodbye that I hadn't managed to say to my dad on the day he died because I missed him dying by one hour: the Tor, which is the centre of my life, my omphalos: Butleigh Monument, where my dad went to say his farewells to his own father.

I don't know how these things happen – but they do. I listen to the dictates of my body and I follow them and some kind of magic seems to happen between my walking feet and the land they walk upon. I am staggered by this more and more often these days. There is an atlas, a map, some multi-dimensional compass in my belly. It speaks to the atoms of my body. They respond. The only other thing I need to do is not think. I have to rein my brain in like a naughty horse, give it some hay, keep it quiet. Then the shy mole of my soul can emerge and lead me on, through the darkness and into it.

With love for now – and also to say that I am developing a score for falling. More of that soon.

21.11.15 From: Phil

Ill Walking Day 2

I was straight way shocked by the dark and bright green waxy leaf with its sharp almond parts; as if it were all eyes. A lizard dropped upon the path. I fell to thinking about totalities. The giant sentinel tree was creaking like a raptor in pain. I never feel at home. In my body whatever it is that is doing this to me, virus or bacteria, is me now. The branches reach in through the bedroom window.

I tap my stick up a small Rise; at the top are entranceways to two houses. The second has parodied the first's pair of white plaster lions with a pair of its own white plaster terriers. Concrete toadstools; a brutalist hallucination. I savour slowly and sink this pleasure into a great slice of moss, ten yards long and two wide, in the generous margins of a driveway. Thick like a fairytale forest, deep darkness there must be beneath. In the tar macadam some wounding and then a hot day has melted its stuff into a black reptile eye.

Best wishes,

24.11.15 From: Alyson

for some strange reason i can't open your latest email – can you send it again please?

thanks,

24.11.15   From: Phil

Ill Walking Day 3

No walk.

Ill Walking Day 4

I pass the house of a recently widowed poet. There are no cars in the drive.

I walk two dead ends of 1960s houses. The kind that people call "characterless". I remember how my dead Dad would sing "little boxes, little boxes". But the houses are creaking and cracking like the lairs of poltergeists.

Two months of illness and it is hard not to feel like a blackbird in darkness. A walking coffin, a fireplace with no fuel. Tempting to see the passing cars as so many machines. The other pedestrians talking about "assignments" and "make a good pair" as programmes working themselves out for someone else. Dead labour and dead leisure.

The first thing I see is the flame. An old gas fire like the one I had in my council flat. A middle-aged man in his 50s reading a magazine. I feel the fug of comfortable cosiness radiating his mild interest, as if his were a popular hobby or an eccentric obsession; ufology before the animal mutilations and conspiracy theories soured it. At the back of the room, holding court over a table of books is a middle-aged man in his 20s who looks up from his pc. A bearded sailor who never left home; in his look I feel a middling quality: a humble suspicion that never quite blossomed into curiosity. Opposite the older middle-aged man is a similarly aged woman at work with materials; she seems to be pasting her long, wiry, salt and pepper hair into a collage.

Monodrama as triptych.

Best wishes,

24.11.15 From: Alyson

I am so sorry to hear you are not well.

There's work in here though – the blackbird in darkness is beautiful. It places us to one side, I think, when we're ill. We're in parallel to the rest of the world, no longer really a part of it. A strange creature, one that doesn't fit with the images that are put across in the advertising hoardings, one that doesn't fit with the mantra of happy, happy, happy shoppers. Even ambition fades away. At times like that I stay in bed and read. Travel to other worlds. Give myself permission to be totally other. It's a bit revolutionary in some ways. Even most medicine is geared to get us back to normal as soon as possible. But what if that soon as possible takes a long time? And what if the normal is never really normal again?

I am so aware that I now have a great lump of metal inside me where my bad old bony hip used to be. There's a dip in the flesh too, as if someone has taken an ice-cream scoop to my thigh muscle and helped themselves to a hefty portion. It looks odd. Looks wrong. So in my new normality I'm a bit deformed. There's an alien substance inside of me and without it I wouldn't be able to walk. I love it and loathe it. Mainly love it, but there is this sneaking suspicion that something unchangeable has happened. That I can never go back to how I was. I am no longer the human being that I have been for the past 50 years.

I am part alien.

The planet is inside of me now in a very tangible way. I have started to press my hand against my hip and feel sure I can feel the metal there. It may not be the case, but imagining it freaks me out. Inside of me is a manmade thing. It is hard. It is not bone. It is metals that have been mined out of the earth. Am I a recipient of quarry from the quarry? Which men and women made the thing that lets me walk along the road without limping? Who are my silent angels? Who are the makers of my body now?

With love,

25.11.15   From: Phil

I forgot to say – your writing about the alien in your leg – it so weaves around what I wrote about my zombie book chapter titled – "The ancient dead in ourselves – the ecological zombie" – if you haven't got the book I can email you the chapter.

Best wishes,

25.11.15 From: Alyson

it's on my list to buy the zombie book –

I wanted to tell you that I went to an exhibition in the Wellcome Institute in London yesterday and saw 'Tibet's Secret Temple'.

There were films of yogic men directing energy into their central channel by doing yogic falls – it was very strange to watch – they would stand up then fall in the cross legged position over and over again.

This is part of a secret energy practice

Other things I liked:

"To realise the essence of consciousness
Approach what you find repulsive
Help whoever you think you cannot help
Let go of anything you are attached to
Go to places that scare you, such as cemeteries….
Be mindful!
Discover the Buddha within yourself"
Mahasiddha Maching Lhabdron (11th century)

and, very appealing to me, in a practice to cut through attachment to the human body they use a trumpet made out of a human thigh bone – this got me thinking about my piece of bone (a femoral head that I persuaded the surgeon to let me keep after the operation) that is quietly

A Conversation

rotting away in a tub of water – at least, my flesh and tendons are rotting away – and I wondered if I might get someone to make it into an ocarina one day – i rather like that idea – transforming my sick old bone into a musical instrument and using it to enlighten myself –

perhaps that's why it horrified me so much when i first saw it – a piece of myself all raw and bloody – i ran out of the room – screaming – here was the part of me that had been sawn off when I was unconscious – what was my hip bone doing in a blue plastic pot? what had the butcher done to me? What was my meat doing there, outside of my skin? How was I ever meant to understand the order of the world again?

Another quote from the exhibition:

"Birth, sickness, ageing and death
flow ever onward, a river without ford or bridge....
have you built yourself a boat?"
     Mahasiddha Padampa Sangye (11th century)

Best,

27.11.15 From: Alyson

yesterday
between trains in Bristol
I stepped out of Temple Meads station to have a coffee by the river.

on the way back
i passed a man with a white stick
a man living somewhere on the spectrum of not being able to see
who was learning to walk out into an open space
with a man who was guiding him

it made me think of you
of the tentative walks
the walks that might be fraught with fear

and it made me cry – i was seeing something really brave

a silent hero
no wars
no medals
no grand walks across the moors
no epic ventures into scenic landscapes –
but a blind man who was about to walk for the first time across the level tarmac of a car park on his own –

his helper stood by his side, talking to him

and then they decided that this was too much, this open terrain, this stretch that he hadn't encountered before,

A Conversation

and so they retreated to the top of the ramp and started from there instead

one man and one long white stick

learning to walk on his own, to trust the eye of the stick as it encountered walls or bumps or potholes

his senses working overtime

and then the sound of all of us passing by, the confusion of that, the thousand things

that were going on around his walking

that connected with his walking – a man being one thing in the midst of so many others –

it was so moving

i was so moved –

and all of this in just the minute or two that it took me to walk up the same ramp,

into Temple Meads, through the barrier and then down into the underground passage

that would give me access to the platform i needed for my train.

best,

A Conversation

28.11.15 From: Phil

There is something brutal about the blue plastic pot. Bad enough the abjection of the inside made outside. But to offer you blue plastic as replacement for your fleshly envelope; cruel. No wonder you screamed. You had to make your own inside to outside. To tame it.

Your words made me see the butcher's display, the window, the show; buildings and cabinets full of flesh and offal. I once wrote a pantomime for a handful of actors; making a virtue of this, I wrote a sketch for the rear half of a pantomime cow, the painted slice through the animal was like one of those charts on butcher's walls where they divide the animal neatly and label each cut. I always thought these were uncanny/funny.

After, a friend curated an exhibition where an artist cast ossuary cases from the ground bones of his uncle (with his permission). I suggested that I would like my skin tanned and made into shoes for others to use so I could continue to journey, so that I could tag along, so that I could impose on others; I am less keen on it now.

I like the idea of visiting cemeteries, even if they do not particularly frighten me (I am minded, always, as a Pip and a pip, a mere seed, of the opening of *Great Expectations*), it is the only comfort I can imagine in death – not my mother's, that she had done everything she wished and was content with the trajectories of those she loved, but of continuing in the only-probabilities of the ever-slowing universe, participating without consciousness as a vital mulch in uncertainty towards an ever-gentler slowing or some as-yet imperceptible spasm that will contract and expand it all again. Shoes are not necessary.

Ill Walking Day 5

I meant to use the visit to the hospital, but the corridors sucked all my intent away and I focused down to the work in hand, despite my pleasure in the weaving through uniformed nurses, orderlies pushing tiny bodies on giant raised beds strung with tubes, and the shamble of visitors; the whole swell of unshowy caring is impressive.

It is not possible for me to have the dislocated sensitivity of a 'drift'; I want too much to be part of this partial enterprise. To get my subjectivity back, I must surrender some of it, it seems, at least for a while. In exchange, the consultants present me with a phantom: all the negative test results point to there being no infection in my body, perhaps; instead I may be suffering from an inflammatory condition brought on by my immune system misreading something as an infection and attacking my body in the absence of anything else to hand.

I am a phantom infection. A bogus rebellion, triggering the occasional cctv reaction, but with no viral meme or bacteriological weapons to offer the struggle. Not the walking dead, but the walking absence.

I will attach the 'ancient' chapter from the zombie book. I hope you like it.

Bests,

29.11.15   From: Phil

Ill Walking Day 6

Feel too ill to walk.

Ill Walking Day 7

There is to be no walking today.

Although the debilitating headache from yesterday has gone, I am saving my energy for a trip to see Exeter City FC. After all, sitting wrapped up in the stands is little different from sitting on the sofa at home with the central heating on.

A few minutes past the arranged time for the taxi, no show, so I ring the taxi firm – 666 666 – "I'm ever so sorry, we're completely backed up" – I put the phone down and set off.

I am unsure. It's a half hour walk. Mostly uphill on the way there. I try to slow myself, but I am anxious not to miss the start. The ground is so familiar and yet today it is as though I am stepping out over unknown territory. I walk methodically up the hill. After five minutes, I realise I have left my analgesic medication in the kitchen. I don't want to go back and I don't want to go a long way round via a shop. I keep going. Not taking my pills is probably what brought on my terrible headache yesterday. I am gambling doubly now.

The light is golden, leaking out of purple clouds, the landscape is location-like. I should not be making this up.

I pass the remnants of an old cut and laid hedge that looks now like untidy shrubbery. I made a performance walk here, having one of the audience run up and down with an ironing board, while I talked about *Stethacanthus*, the extinct genus of shark with ironing board shapes rather than triangular fins that populated the Carboniferous oceans in which the geology of the hill was formed. As I reach the top of the hill, I have no real sense of my body; the sky has darkened and it rains for a while.

Today, 'walking ill' feels like a technical exercise. I find it hard to displace my concentration. I distract myself to let the motor run without too much variation. I do not attend to tangents. I become target-oriented.

I am surprised at how easily I complete the mile and a half. I am also aware that I have approached but not passed a point of no return.

The match kicks off as I take my seat. It is a very high quality game; the opposition, Bristol Rovers, are on top form and Exeter work very hard to keep them out. There are numerous attacks, shots and saves. I am surprised that the match reaches half-time without a score. Exeter are struggling. I feel fine. The adrenaline rush of the match medicates me for the time being. I chat to my neighbouring season ticket holders about the match. Half way through the second half I begin to shiver, rain is falling like glass spears and the wind rises. Exeter have begun to get back into match, creating more chances, but still facing assaults on their own goal. My head begins to ache. I begin to wonder at walking home in the downpour. No taxi home now. Seven minutes from fulltime and Bristol Rovers score. It is almost a relief. Exeter must fight back rather than hang on; I yell more.

A Conversation

Exeter attack and attack, the ball bounces around in the Bristol Rovers' penalty area. We miss the goal from a perfectly positioned free kick. Injury time, the match is almost over. The ball bounces out of play by where I sit, very close to the pitch. Aaron Davies, one of our players collects the ball and as he bends to pick up it I growl in his ear, "keep going, Aaron, keep going!" and in the following play Exeter cross the ball once more towards Rovers' goal, the ball is deflected back, Davies sweeps the ball on over his own head and one of our young local players, Jamie Reid, come up through the youth system, volleys the ball through a reeling thicket of players into the net.

I leap to my feet and reach to the sky with fists and gestures.

The game ends. I have no headache. Given the informality of lower league football, to my left some young members of the Bristol Rovers playing staff have been watching and they pass me now. One of them catches my eye and raises his. "You deserved to win that", I say and squeeze his arm. He nods. I clap the players off and climb the steps to leave the stadium.

As I leave I expect to meet our Head of Football, a former England player, and I think that I will say to him: "never say die". Then I remember that this is the spot where I saw him so nearly die, a heart attack, looked into his eyes and saw a man knowing how much trouble his body is in, saved by surgery and a three week induced coma. This is where I stood with the rest of the stand and applauded as he was carried out. Then turned and sat to watch the rest of the match.

Outside the rain has stopped. Sunlight has gone. The vehicle headlights flicker and stretch on the wet roads. I am not walking but floating. I know that I can only rely on this unreality for a while. I notice that I am struggling on the one hill home as I reach the peak; mildly hallucinating, on the down incline my legs become puppet-like. I recognise this feeling from the end of very long walks when I am at the edge of what I can do – a twenty plus mile walk carrying a plinth in Belgium, Jess Allen's equally lengthy 'Tilting At Windmills' walk up many Welsh hills – I dream walk, faint walk, see things that are slightly 'beside' what should be there.

No automatism is left in my legs, I operate them; they flop up and down on strings of will. Having reached home, I take my pills and rush to do as little as possible. I sleep for eleven hours, sweating and sweating.

1.12.15 From: Phil

a little more 'Ill Walking' Day 8

Yesterday I was the route and the terrain – not the walker.

After three attempts by two nurses, a vein was found to accept the cannula and I was wheeled into a treatment room. The heart monitor was clipped to a thumb. The sedative injected and the acerbic anaesthetic sprayed onto the back of my throat.

When the professor had described the procedure, I had imaged it as a diagram, so now I stood outside my body and watched the tiny tube with its camera head and jaws worming in an out of the inverted tree of my bronchia.

A cave system anesthetised on a water table.

I was reminded of how Anjali Jay, who worked as an 'outside eye' on my 'The Crab Walks' performances, had described my body, up close to audiences crammed into the beach huts where I performed, as "becoming the map of your journeys".

Far more extended than the brief hallucinatory chaos of my first bronchoscopy, which was rather like flashing on the album cover of 'Court of the Crimson King', this time I seem to be inside myself for much, much longer.

I am a set of instinctive reactions and spasms. I don't have a body, I am verb. Coughing, rasping, gagging, gasping and wheezing desperately as there is either the most limited route to air or none at all. What remains of that calm bronchial map is now seething and fitting, synthetic tubes and inflamed tunnels exploring each other; the cave system is full of well-intentioned monsters, hurting to help.

"Pain?"

"Tiny." And it really is. What is larger is the melancholy of rooms and beds and screens and corridors. I am writing this sentence so that its final word brings me to the front door ready to walk. Having typed the full stop, the phone rings; one of the consultants checking on my symptoms.

Ill Walking Day 9

I intend to walk in response to your email the other day about seeing the man walking with the white stick. Since then I have had some unworked-out idea about wanting to walk as if I were a stick, or as if a wheel on a wheelchair. To walk as if I was the prosthesis. I have no idea what this means and hope that the walk might find it out for me.

I worry that it might be presumptive and disrespectful to anyone using these things.

Outside I am distracted by the noise and clutter of escaping the house, and then by turning sharp left into a cul-de-sac that I have never walked before. Very close to our house, it lies within the university campus, but mostly made up of private houses. I am surprised by just how big they are; some must have 15 or 20 rooms in them. Many of them are in gated clusters or protected behind forbidding walls. I note how deep and green with moss the pavements between the houses are, as if no one ever walks them, and I ponder on this strange debility of the rich.

Best wishes,

1.12.15 From: Alyson

A Score for Falling Down:

> When you fall, you fall through all the points of the body.
>
> Through all of its horizontalities, all the places where it seemed to belong.
>
> Falling takes you down through the body of yourself,
>
> you are a rapidly descending lift,
>
> the building around you gives way as you fall.

A Conversation

You collapse.

You unreel each rib and send it down to the ground.

The structure that held you upright gives way.

The skeleton gives way.

The muscles give way and surrender to gravity, to falling, to toppling.

The grid of existence – you no longer have a reference point on it.

For the duration of the fall you are unhooked untethered from everything human, everything familiar.

You have not only exited the vertical way of being, you have also exited a way of being understood as human.

Fallen, you become something we have no name for.

You are in a sphere of transformation.

We usually try to exit this place as quickly as possible.

To stand again, to rise.

The fallen body and the ground where we fall are not lingered over – they are perceived as aberrant, other, unwanted.

Yes.

Unwanted in the extreme.

Despised.

There is a musical score/grid to accompany this. X

A Conversation

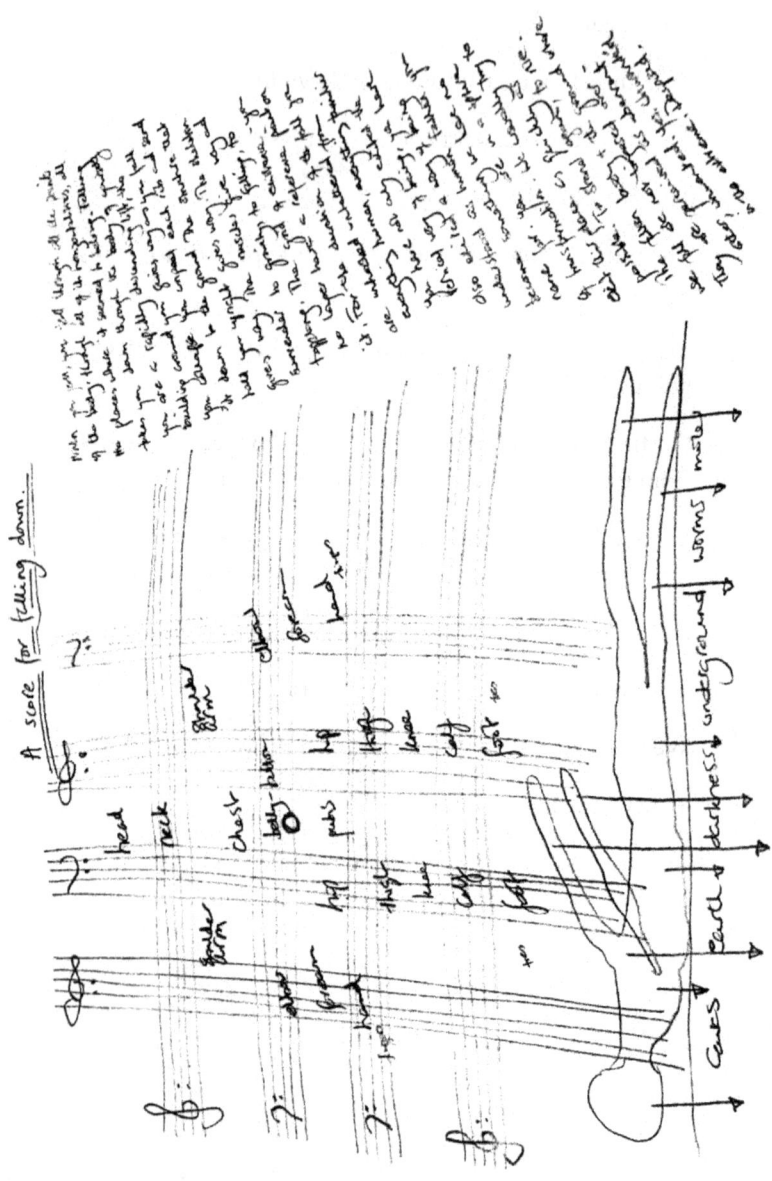

5.12.15   From: Phil

Returning to the places where we fell.... I think you are right.... why do we not do that? I wrote some mini-scores for falls.... I might try and write some more.

Scores for a fall:

Hubris fall: slip on the lost pen with which you had intended to write that difficult second novel.

Politician's fall: trip over a missile you understandably mistook for a conscience.

Phenomenological fall: stand exactly still on slim harbour steps and let the algae bring you down, splintering, on your elbows.

Fortean fall: race towards the parapet where dogs inexplicably leap to their deaths, trip up on the way.

Structuralist fall: stumble on the carpet you chose for its pattern.

Geological fall: lost in a thought experiment, trip on a bump in the tarmac beneath which the mantle is carrying out enquiries of its own.

Exemplary fall: on a walk with walking artists, slip on a gutter slab of granite and pitch onto your chest. Bounce back up.

Histrionic fall: have an audience hold you suspended.

Ambiguous fall: be rigid and catatonic until the authorities carry you away in a flight through public space.

Best wishes,

A Conversation

8.12.15 From: Alyson

I watched Selma on Sunday and was struck by walking as protest.

Not going for a walk, nipping out to the shops, hiking in a park, trekking, sauntering up to the viewpoint,

but walking for something that's believed in,

moving our two feet on the ground as a way of saying something that can't be said in any other way.

The impact of that.

I thought of how just a few people walking together for a purpose can start to change the world.

So low-tech it's almost laughable.

Two feet walking at the pace of the human – one step in front of the next, and in a way no distance too great.

The slowness of the walk.

The deep humility of it.

The absence of rush, or anything other than belief propelling the human body onwards.

And then how they were struck down.

How the police came with batons and struck them down.

How the police came on horseback and struck them down again and again.

People with no weapons, no violent intent – just their two walking feet and a need for social justice and equality.

There are histories in our feet that get forgotten.

I wish we kept the shoes of great walkers.

Perhaps I will start a shoe museum for that. The shoes of walkers and protesters.

A refuge for the footwear after it has served its purpose and is worn out.

I think it would be a fabulous thing to do.

What do you think about a museum of walker's shoes?

And how are you?

Best,

18.12.15 From: Phil

Having recently co-written a play about Martin Luther King this struck me very hard. There was a terrible dilemma for MLK; many, many of their marches were attacked and yet had no 'effect' – not all of them were covered by national media. Where the cops and politicians were canny, they were not attacked but protesters were arrested and beaten up out of sight, and then there was no pressure on the government. So MLK and his team had to knowingly generate violence from the Southern racist cops in front of national media in order to put pressure on the Kennedys in the White House. It was not easy to lead – aside from the ever-present threat of death – non-violent resistance turned out to be more complicated than anyone expected.

Did you see the protest of shoes in Paris?

When shoes are kept in museums they tend to be shown as ornaments or examples of a moment of cultural design – but a museum of shoes as things of the walk and the walkers – yes.

I don't seem to have been Ill Walking over the last few days – I have been walking in a different way – I have been feeling somewhat better, but I'm not well, and this can catch me out, a couple of days ago I tried to walk into town (15 minutes usually) and got into trouble on the way back, experiencing some odd feelings and exhaustion. Once home I sat immobile on the sofa and watched hours and hours of 'The Bridge' and 'Fargo'. Today I walked into the town and back and I was fine. Anyway, I have written about this walking and attach it.

Best wishes,

>
> There is a deluded impostor living in my body,
>
> He believes he's getting well again,
>
> But it's my body that's getting better at being ill.
>
> As smooth as well-rehearsed chorus boys we are, my body and him,

A Conversation

Indulging our morbid choreographies, unselfconsciously,

But there's neither thing nor manner that is well, phenomenologically.

When I catch my body in the morning mirror

It's my father's; the one in the care home, the one at the end.

Dead is the seventeen stone dancer I was, full of thickness I'd kneaded,

And wanted to be. No more that erratic; gone that walking menhir

I'd still looked forward to having words with, to hearing make poetry from inside stone.

That future doesn't happen now. And I don't wish to do anything I've done before.

I'm not that one. I am a skip under sodium. Walking sticks and tent pegs grip

Under my calves and thighs, forcing them into corners;

Rucksack claws pin my shoulders on the yellow, withered frame.

I'm not sure who you think is writing this anymore. Or how sick.

But let me assure myself that, inside this darkening landscape,

I am driving the auto-immune with the lights full beam

And my impostor beside me in the passenger seat, drawing maps

With its fingertips in steam on the windscreen, and when we are well again

We'll ditch this thing and set off, thinly, across the scarified fields of change.

6.1.16 From: Alyson

Wow. The poem is amazing.

Really striking and moving and sad and disturbing and intriguing.

It is a long time since you sent this email and i didn't reply.

I appreciate your patience.

The way these communications move between us with a rhythm of their own.

Not to be rushed or slowed.

Just as they are – which is so difficult sometimes, especially in this medium where waiting a day for a response can seem agonising.

My mum has been very ill.

A Conversation

I have been walking hospital corridors for the past three weeks.

My mum has always been ill – at least, that's how it seems.

The hospital corridors are very familiar to me. They are like old friends.

O, here we go again. The green, non-slip lino/rubbery stuff on the stairs. It's got little raised circles in it, as if circular insects might have buried into the material when it was being made, and now live in their strange universe on the hospital stairs, getting beaten down each day by the footsteps of visitors.

O, hello corridors with wards branching off on each side. One ward, Conservator (that my mum accidentally called Conservatoire in a text message) was, really, a hell destination. Crowded, smelling of urine, a woman with large, almost unrecognisable breasts exposed on my right, a young boy with a tube in his nose sleeping on the left, a swirling mass of old and young and ill, ill, ill people – not a conservatoire at all, no music, nothing like that, except the music of beeping machines, moans, barely repressed screams. Thankfully mum was not here – on the neurology and endocrine ward – instead she was on Montacute, up in the new wing, in a room of her own.

O swish along the corridors of art. Thank god for hospital art. In the new wing there's Nash, Long – even a Hodgkin print. I stop and look at these but mostly I waltz past all the pretty pictures. Unremittingly glad they're there, but not in the mood to stop and stare and study.

These walks are strange walks. As soon as I'm making them I'm also wishing I wasn't. The fetid air. Incumbent germs. The compulsory scoosh of antiseptic hand gel before entering a ward, hands wet and glistening. The landscape is irrepressibly right-angled. All of it. Every possible curve ironed out. Staff wander by in strange uniforms. Odd paper hats on the heads of men and women who work in the theatres. Gurneys squeaking here and there. Croc-footed theatre staff. Uniformed staff. Patients with tubes and wheelchairs; looks of resignation.

My eyes look out as much as they can. My feet carry me wherever I need to go, but often I'm not there at all. Part of me is flying high over the Quantocks. Out there over the green hills. Part of me is lifting up like the helicopter that lands or takes off out the front of the hospital. Straight up, into the cold fresh air, up where the clouds are, up where there's no one else apart from other carers or people who just need to get away for a bit.

How is your walking now, in 2016?

11.1.16 From: Phil

I am so sorry to hear about your Mum. There is something strange about the routine when someone is very ill. You do the same things, the same things happen. But you know that change can creep up on you, or accelerate, very suddenly. It gives repetition a strange suspendedness that is not far from an inappropriate suspense.

I was seen by a Registrar in hospital today. I should have said to him "I haven't been able to write about being ill or limping recently, what can you do for me?" but instead I asked about my weariness: he said to me that I should think of my illness as being equivalent to those astronauts on early space flights before they realised that they had to exercise. I have completely deconditioned my body. Accidentally, I have conducted a kind of blankness onto my body. Time to start walking again.

I couldn't write about being ill or getting better. I wrote about plenty of other things over the new year: academic papers... and so on. But I wrote something today and I attach that.

Your writing of the visits to your Mum is remarkable. I can almost not bear to read it. It affects my skin. I'm too much there.

What are we going to do with these writings? How is your hip? Is it time to stop writing about these things and move on? What do you think?

Best wishes,

A Conversation

I am not dead today and David Bowie did not die

A body did not fall from the lip of the gods

Or through an industrialised sky.

From the cardboard balustrade of the hippodrome

I am not hanging today.

My soul was saved by the body of the minister's daughter,

The bottle of English sherry did not shatter through the skin it was hiding in.

I am not dead today I know because the letter from the hospital says:

"this gentleman remains a mystery" and "I will discuss him further with Bill Lusty".

I am not dead today and David Bowie did not die,

I know because there are so many lies

And all my spilled blood ends up in laboratories.

I gave up fighting ground control and gravitational pull.

I've been making my own spatial turn around the arm of our settee,

Hiding from recovery inside recovery, on a space walk round my capsule,

For month on month ticking the days and critiquing moonscape.

Suddenly in a lull my organs were floating free and the rest of me

Spinning like a thin black star of embroidery.

I did not die today and nor did David Bowie, we talked our way in and out

Of different shifts, escaping on each other's withered stilts of skin.

11.1.16 From: Alyson

good questions

and great poem.

answers have I none but here are suggestions:

the first thing that came to mind is: do we have enough interesting/relevant/connected materials to conceive of a pamphlet that would be a conversation of sorts? not an interview, but two people musing around an idea? I rather like the idea of conversation pamphlets

if this is the case

then yes, we should move on to something else next, a new conversation, but should we first review and see if what we've done so far has any legs or if it has sunk into the quicksand?

and what are your thoughts on these questions?

11.1.16 From: Phil

I like the idea of a conversation pamphlet – perhaps we could play with whose voice is whose....

So, yes, to reviewing what we have... What is the best way to do that?

Is there a subtle and incremental way? Or do we both – separately – do something brash and big with the parts? Or do we talk the structure of the conversation first?

12.1.16 From: Alyson

good questions – the words that jump out and appeal to me are brash and big, but i'm not sure what i do with that

i'm in exeter at the beginning of february and i wonder if we might have a little time to play with the material?

i'm foraging around in the dark here, which is always fun

and thinking we might compose the conversation like a piece of music -

where it doesn't necessarily have to be consequential

but, like a child, i usually need a big floorspace to have all the bits of paper in front of me, so that i can dance with them in a way

thanks for calling a halt by the way – i just go on writing forever!

best, p.s. i hope you are feeling better.....

An Alphabet of Falling: Alyson & Phil

Accident: what we experience as a moment when the ground deceives us can be a way of being for many people who constantly expect to be tripped up and humiliated.

Broken: the gap that opens up, as we slip, between what we thought we were and what we think we may be about to become.

Change: falling changes our relationships to the ground and to ourselves.

Down: how we feel, unless we acknowledge that slipping up is possible too.

Everything: the ground is always beneath you. In everything you do. Bath, shopping, eating, drinking. It's there. Under you. Waiting.

Flamingo: when my hip aches, I rest all my weight in my left leg and tilt to one side.

Ground: a friend in a fall, a traitor when it halts it.

Intimidate: a fall can intimidate.

Jump: an awakening that happens when there is one more or one less step than you expected.

Kinetics: a theoretical training that does not prepare you.

Learn: in the end, we learn about the ground that we walk on. How variable it is, how the same ground is different for different people.

Lie: the aftermath of a fall.

Mound: a space of sacred and/or sexual falling.

New: a change of your relationship to the ground changes you – this is a revelation about the ground but you also potentially come up with a new body, a new awareness of your body.

O!: part of the liturgy of falling. Call: O! Response: (that's up to everyone else).

Piss Alley: where I heard an old lover had died. My legs crumbled. I was suddenly down on the ground, back against a wall, the stink of piss in my nostrils. I love this place now. It is an unmarked memorial.

Political: if you help me stand back up after I have fallen, you are making a political act.

Quest: the thing that comes before a fall and the challenge that comes after.

Resistance: kick the stone and it kicks back.

Stone: one of many partners in the dance of tripping, stumbling and falling.

An Alphabet

Transgression: I want to crawl, I want to be someone who has fallen.

Uneven: most falls relate to the ground being uneven.

Vulnerable: I can break.

When: when you go down, you bring up something from the ground.

X: marks the spots where you will fall next.

why: the question you are rarely able to answer in retrospect.

Zeno's paradox: no one ever completes a fall, for all bodies, when dropping, are always a half of the shrinking distance to the ground, and then a half again; we get closer and closer but we never reach our destiny.

Postscript: Phil

I have these temporary employments, occasionally. Contractors that need a writer to compose some text for them; reports, inscriptions, all sorts. Remember, somebody was paid for "they're tasty, tasty, very very tasty, they're very tasty", it didn't just happen.

On this occasion the brief was a little indistinct, so I booked a cheap hotel and caught the train for a site visit. I traversed the new development where I was due to be working; spoke, without appointments, to some friendly site managers, archaeologists and museum staff. Learned about the many corpses from ancient graves dug up and shifted to lay the foundations. Started to get an odd feeling, checked the map and spotted the name of a neighbouring road; the scene of notorious murders some years back. Guiltily, but feeling somehow obliged, I walked that way, felt the eyes of locals scanning over me, speeded up, down the cleared and levelled land where the bodies had been buried, and tripped; on smooth, flat asphalt I stumbled as if something reached from the ground and held me by the heel for a moment.

I was shocked that there was no shrine, no mark at all, for the victims there. Shocked more to see that the road was named on my tourist map; and learn that that was to stop ghouls like me bothering the residents for directions.

The 'ground' or 'grounds' for being – our existential 'grounds' – are not the same for everyone; there is never any such thing as a 'level playing field'. A place where one body is safe, another is not, even though nothing has changed but the identity of the person present – that is a sign of 'grounds'.

Stumbling, falling and tripping are not necessarily a result of the actions of the person thrown out of their stride, nor are they necessarily a result of the environmental specifics of the place where the disruption takes place; but they are always the work of the 'grounds'.

If you want to find a wilderness, go and crawl in public.

So, it is that every stumble and every break from a smooth trajectory through the city or across fields – calamitous like my mother's twisting a knee in a ploughed furrow, or momentary like so many of my own – is an invitation to consider the unevenness of the 'playing field', the conspiracy of malevolent materials (at least, that's how they might appear to themselves if they had any concept of good and evil) and social relations founded on the premises of patriarchy and property's dominance.

As we wobble, momentarily embarrassed, or hammer the granite pavement slab with a soft shoulder point, it is our painful duty, no less than Orpheus's in his quest to the underworld, to come back from below *with something*. Not to look back at what might have caused our disruption; but to look deeper (down inside ourselves, or into the guts of the world) to know why we don't all fall in the same way. Why even in accidents, the consequences are different from person to person, identity to identity, class to class, appearance to appearance.

One of our emails describes how a pioneer of Butoh spent time living on his hands and knees among pigs, before standing up and devising a new kind of dance in full knowledge of what is beneath. I am sure the story is correct, but I like the fact that I cannot verify it yet; that I can stay sceptical of what sounds so right.

For the limping person, flat ground is uneven. For the limping person, walking with one foot in the gutter is an allowance to do something they didn't even know had

Postscript

been forbidden. A tiny child's falls are taken for granted as part of the process of walking; an adult's falls are humiliating, as if adults ever stopped learning how to walk. We tend to get to our feet as quickly as possible, editing away the shock. In 2008, on a walk led by walkwalkwalk (Gail Burton, Clare Qualmann and Serena Korda) I slipped on a wet granite kerbstone, plunging into the road and bounced off my chest and straight back to my feet, too embarrassed to take a pause in my pontificating.

In 2013, quite by chance, I began to work with dancers and choreographers. I was struck by the way their toes were. Unlike people – like me – who spend their lives in boots and shoes, their toes spread out across the surfaces they move on rather than squeezed together like a crowd encircled by hyenas. I had always feared stubbing my toes, but in the warm months I began to walk barefoot at home. As in the rehearsal studio, I began to choose where I placed my toes, sole and heel for each step, rather than simply throwing my foot out ahead of me. In a few months the spread of my toes and the strategic shape of my feet and my thinking had changed. For all my previous walking, I was learning again how to walk and it changed my body and my mind.

I never stubbed my toes again, but I did not stop falling. It did change my attitude though. Slipping as I ran down the stairs at home, my feet flying from under me, I distinctly remember thinking, in mid-air, "this is interesting, I wonder how this will play out". I landed on my back with barely a bruise.

Now, as a result of the corporeal and mental challenges I describe in this book, I am not so sure if I will dance again. Not because I can't, but because the 'grounds' have changed for me and I will have to change them again.

So, what can we bring back when we fall?

Postscript

Nothing very solid or dogmatic, I suspect. Those things will wither and fade in the upright position. Rather it is a knowing that is impossible to demonstrate, an intuition of deceptions and unfairness that we will never prove by enough examples. In that sense it is a kind of faith; not Kierkegaard's 'leap to faith', but our 'fall to faith'. In our helplessness – if we will accept it, and any offers of help that come along – we will feel the cold, dark mechanics of ideology; the anatomy, on the slab, of ideas and images that shape the world unfairly, that split the world along the easiest and most banal fractures. This is a dark work, an alchemical unworking performed not by the transforming of the body but by the traducing of the body, a rare chance to bring a knowing of the 'grounds' up to its surface; it is the return of a repressed knowing of that which cannot be known, a sense of what works in us when we are not aware, when we are not moral, when we are not social: "there's something of the nocturnal Eurydice of the underworld that will be lost to [Orpheus] in the daylight.... He wants to see the elusive dimension of her that can't be seen. He wants to see her ... when she is invisible" (Josh Cohen, 2013, 'The Private Life', *Granta*, 37-8).

When you next fall, stay down for a while, see what comes.

Then, when you get to your feet again, rather than relying on your body's natural approximations of space, choose your steps, not anxiously but in an excited kind of wariness; and, with each pace, a little more undo the 'grounds' that tripped you up.

Appendix 1

Some of the other practitioners and writers in this field (mentioned on p.15) include:

The late **Sue Porter** was an activist and researcher interrogating what "walking" is:
http://bit.ly/philyson01 and http://bit.ly/philyson02

Dee Heddon had been working with Sue on opposing normative walking.

Amy Sharrocks falls:
http://bit.ly/philyson04

Alison Lloyd walks mountains and writes about falling:
http://bit.ly/philyson05

Gail Burton has done crawling performances – round a lake – up a church aisle:
http://bit.ly/philyson06

Linda Cracknell broke her leg:
http://bit.ly/philyson07

William Pope.L produced 'The Beautiful', a choreographed crawl performance in 2015:
http://bit.ly/philyson08

Queer academic and performer **Nando Messias** walks as a sissy:
http://bit.ly/philyson09 and http://bit.ly/philyson10

Appendix 2: Alyson

The image on the back cover is of my hip bone. Formally known as a femoral head, this part of the bone connects with the pelvis and when healthy allows the leg to achieve a full range of movement. When a hip replacement operation is carried out, the femoral head is sawn off. I requested that I be allowed to keep my bone after the operation. The first surgeon I saw refused to discuss this and told me it was impossible. The second surgeon was not only open to this suggestion, but amenable to making sure it happened. After surgery, my friend Jan took the bone home (it was starting to smell in the cabinet next to my bed in a warm hospital) and put it in a freezer compartment.

Two months later, Jan and I opened the bag that contained the frozen bone and defrosted it. At this point, there were remnants of tendon and muscle attached to it. In order to clean it, I put it in a pot with cold water and Ecover washing-up liquid. This process is known as cold water maceration and causes minimum damage to the bone. However, the process is slow and the water becomes smelly quite quickly. I then decided to bury the bone in the garden. I dug a deep hole, not wanting dogs or badgers to sniff it out, and popped the bone in. On top of where it was buried, I made a circle of stones.

Nine months after my operation, I dug the bone up again. Worms, maggots and other things that live in dark soil had successfully cleaned the bone of flesh.

Acknowledgements

Alyson would like to thank Fiona Hamilton for her insightful reading of the text; Jan Blake for her support and for taking care of her sawn-off bone when she was recovering from her operation; Mr Eastaugh-Waring for being an amazing surgeon and having enough imagination to respond positively to her request to keep her hip bone; Mercedes Nunez and Grizel Luttman-Johnson for looking after her when she was learning to walk again; and Trevor Burgess for pointing her in the direction of the work of Michael Andrews.

Phil would like to thank Mari Sved for reading and commenting on an early draft, and the nurses, technicians, doctors and consultants of the National Health Service for all their care during his recent illness.

The publishers would like to thank James Hyman of the James Hyman Gallery, London for permission to reproduce the cover image: 'A Man Who Suddenly Fell Over' by Michael Andrews. (The full credit appears on the copyright page.)

About the Authors

Dr Phil Smith is a prolific writer, performer, urban mis-guide, dramaturg [for TNT Munich], artist-researcher and academic. He has written or co-written over 100 professionally produced plays, and created and performed in numerous site-specific theatre projects, often with Exeter-based Wrights & Sites, of which he is a core member. He has collaborated more recently with choreographers Melanie Kloetzel, Siriol Joyner and Jane Mason. He is a site artist for Tracing the Pathway's Groundwork project in Milton Keynes.

Photo: Rachel Sved

He is Associate Professor (Reader) in the School of Humanities and Performing Arts at Plymouth University.

Phil has published papers in *Studies in Theatre and Performance, Performance Research, Cultural Geographies*, and *New Theatre Quarterly,* co-authored a range of Mis-Guides with his fellow members of Wrights & Sites, and written/co-written many other books including: *On Walking…and Stalking Sebald; Walking's New Movement; Enchanted Things; Mythogeography; Counter-Tourism: The Handbook; A Sardine Street Book of Tricks; Walking, Writing and Performance; A Footbook of Zombie Walking* and the novel *Alice's Dérives in Devonshire.*

Fuller details of his work can be found at:

www.triarchypress.net/smithereens

Dr Alyson Hallett is a prize-winning poet. Her collections include *On Ridgegrove Hill* (Atlantic Press), *Suddenly Everything* (Poetry Salzburg), *The Stone Library* (Peterloo Poets), *Towards Intimacy*, (Queriendo Press). Co-authored books include *6 Days in Iceland* (Dropstone Press) and *365* (Agre Press). Alyson is a Hawthornden Fellow, and she was the UK's first poet to be resident in a geography department at the University of Exeter, Cornwall Campus with an award from the Leverhulme Trust.

Photo: Sean Malyon

Alyson has also published a book of short stories, *The Heart's Elliptical Orbit* (Solidus Press), a play for Radio 4, *Dear Gerald*, drama for Sky Television, *Agony*, an audio-diary for Radio 4, *Nature: Migrating Stones*, and academic research into relationships between poetry, poet and landscape, *Geographical Intimacy* (Amazon).

Collaboration with artists, dancers, musicians, scientists is core to her work: she has a poem carved into a pavement in Bath; text etched into a library window in Bristol; poetry carved into a guide stone in the Peak District; words carved into an installation of boulders at Falmouth University.

She has received several awards from Arts Council England, enabling her to create and curate her international poetry-as-public-art project, *The Migration Habits of Stones*. She has sited five stones with poetry carved into them (by letter carver Alec Peever) in England, Scotland, U.S.A. and Australia.

Alyson is an Advisory Fellow with the Royal Literary Fund and a visiting lecturer at Falmouth University and UWE. More details of her work can be found at:

www.thestonelibrary.com

About the Publisher

Triarchy Press is a small, independent publisher of interesting, original and alternative thinking about:

- organisations and government, financial and social systems – and how to make them work better

- human beings and the ways in which they participate in the world – moving, walking, thinking, dreaming, suffering and loving.

Triarchy has published several books on the subject of radical, performative or alternative walking (by authors like Roy Bayfield, Claire Hind, Clare Qualmann and Phil Smith) – see **www.triarchypress.net/walking** for details.

Further details of all our books can be found at:

www.triarchypress.net

www.ingramcontent.com/pod-product-compliance
Lightning Source LLC
Chambersburg PA
CBHW071009160426
43193CB00012B/1985